COVIDinners:

Adventures in Quarantine Dining

Katie M. Zeigler

When the shelter-in-place order was announced in March 2020, I found myself desperate to find some way to keep our spirits up through the crisis.

So, on my kitchen whiteboard, I began drawing silly little daily dinner menus that quickly garnered the attention of family and friends.

Irreverent and, at times, downright ridiculous, I hope these menus keep you laughing and well-fed!

Sending you lots of love,
Katie

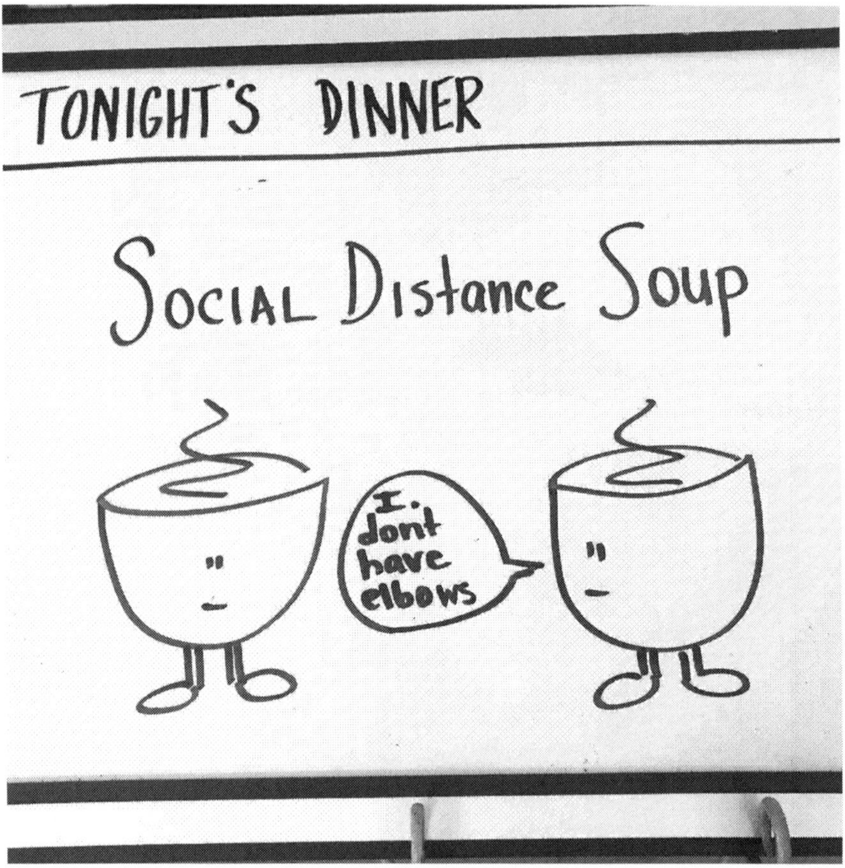
TONIGHT'S DINNER
SOCIAL Distance Soup
I. dont have elbows

#reallylongspoons

#oneflewoverthecouscousnest

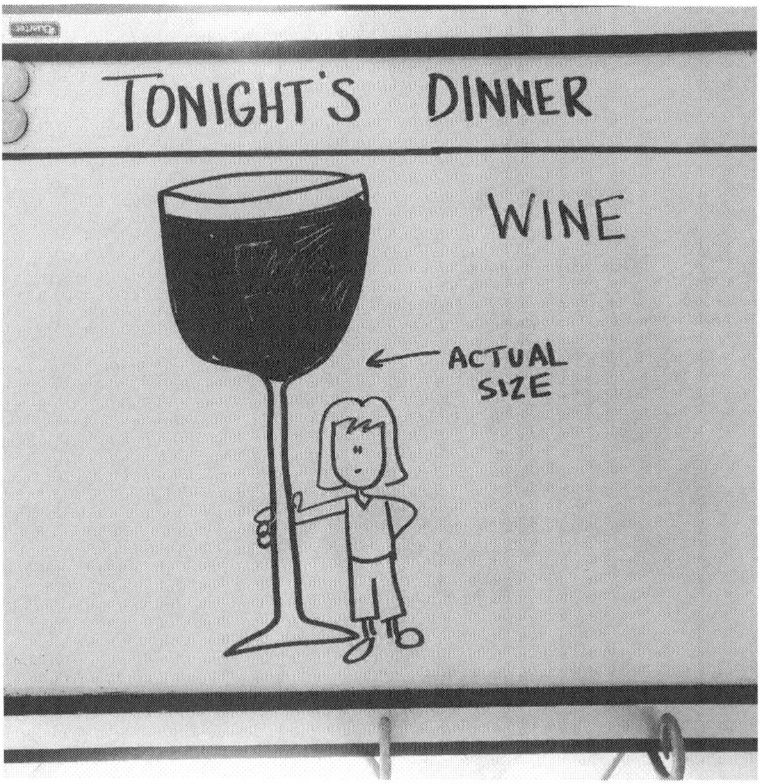
TONIGHT'S DINNER
WINE
ACTUAL SIZE

#grapesarefruit

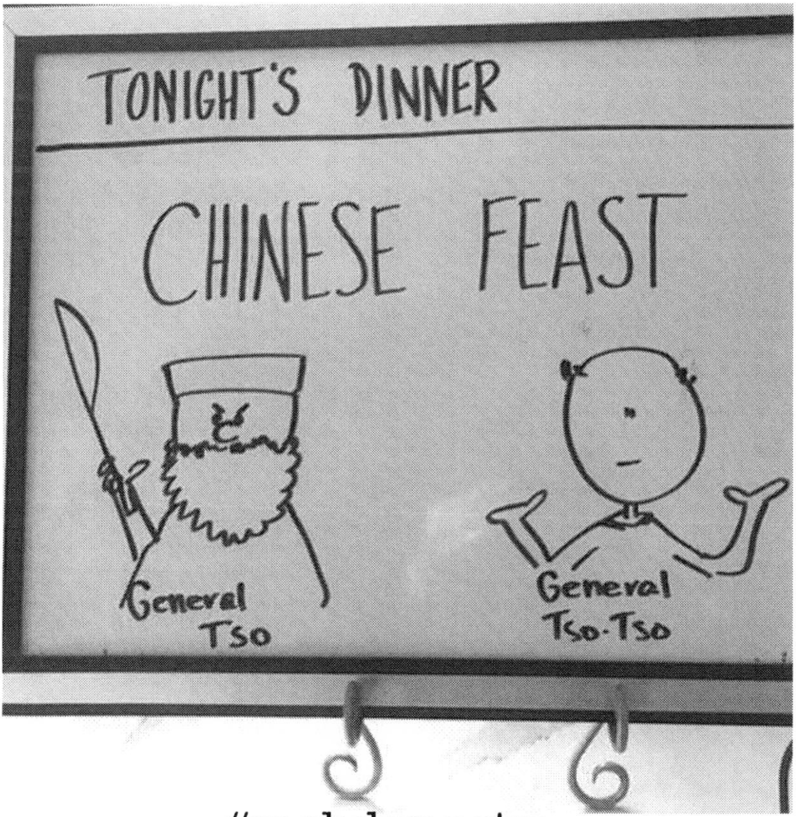
TONIGHT'S DINNER
CHINESE FEAST
General
Tso
General
Tso-Tso

#mehdynasty

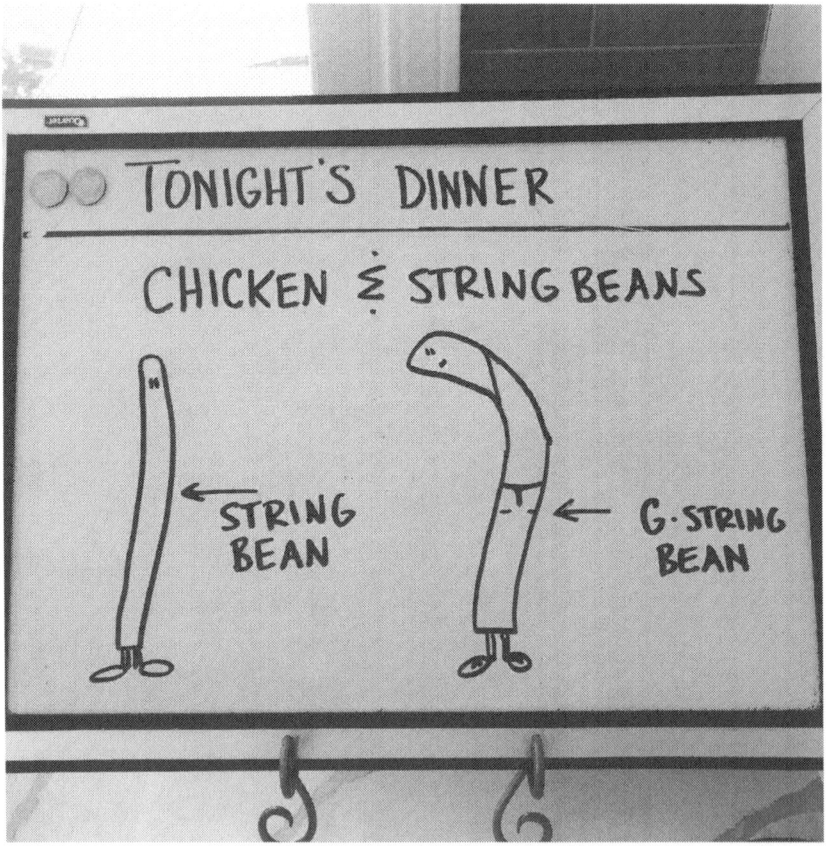
TONIGHT'S DINNER
CHICKEN & STRING BEANS
STRING BEAN
G-STRING BEAN

#GLUTEnfree

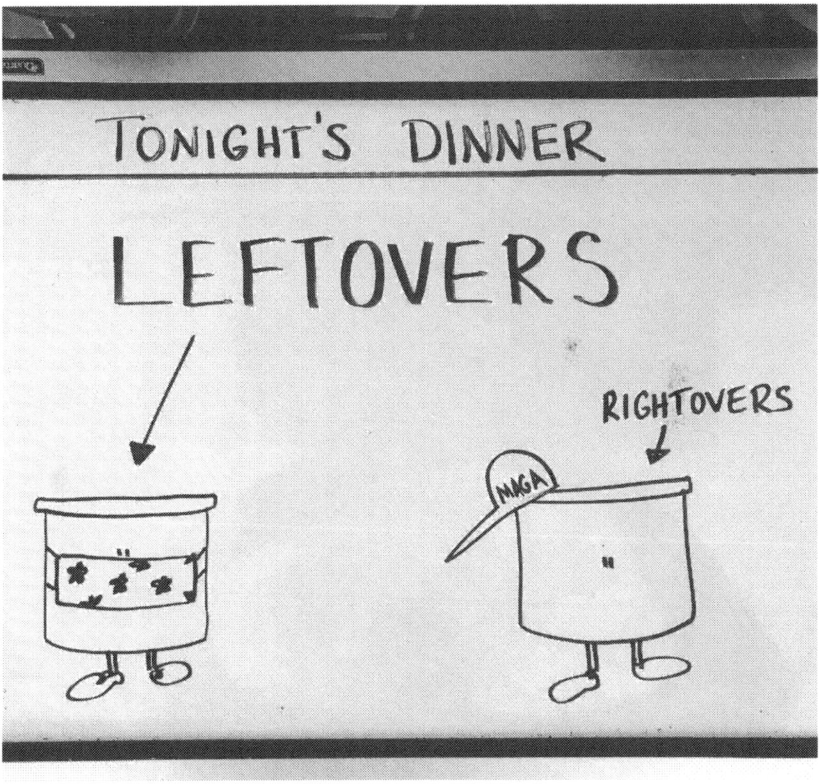
TONIGHT'S DINNER
LEFTOVERS
RIGHTOVERS
MAGA

#politicalories

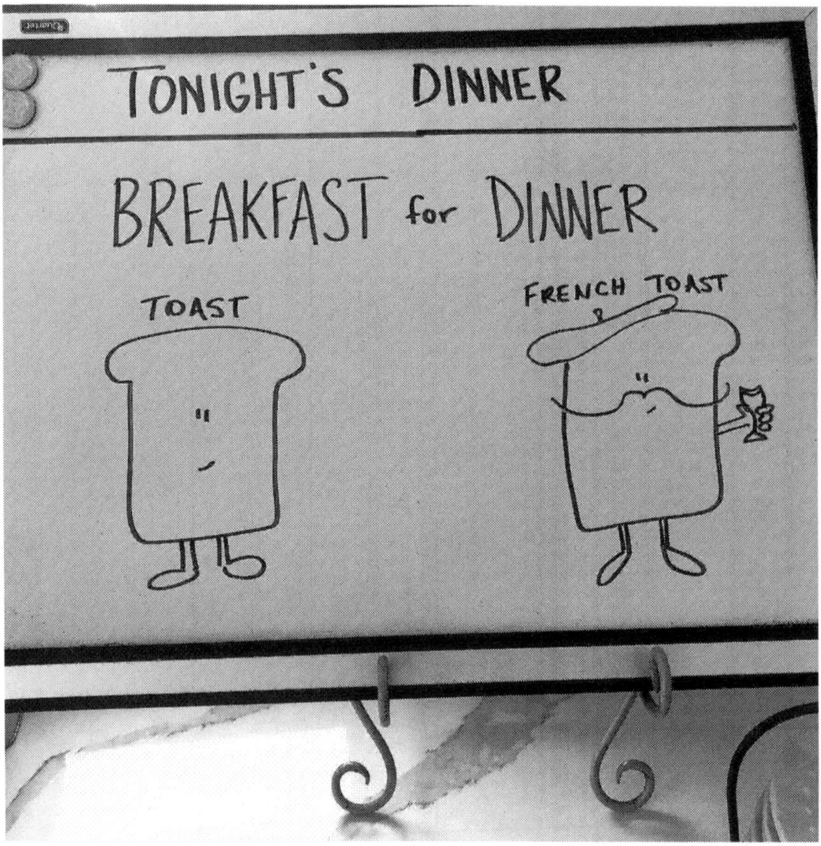
TONIGHT'S DINNER
BREAKFAST for DINNER
TOAST
FRENCH TOAST

#joiedevirus

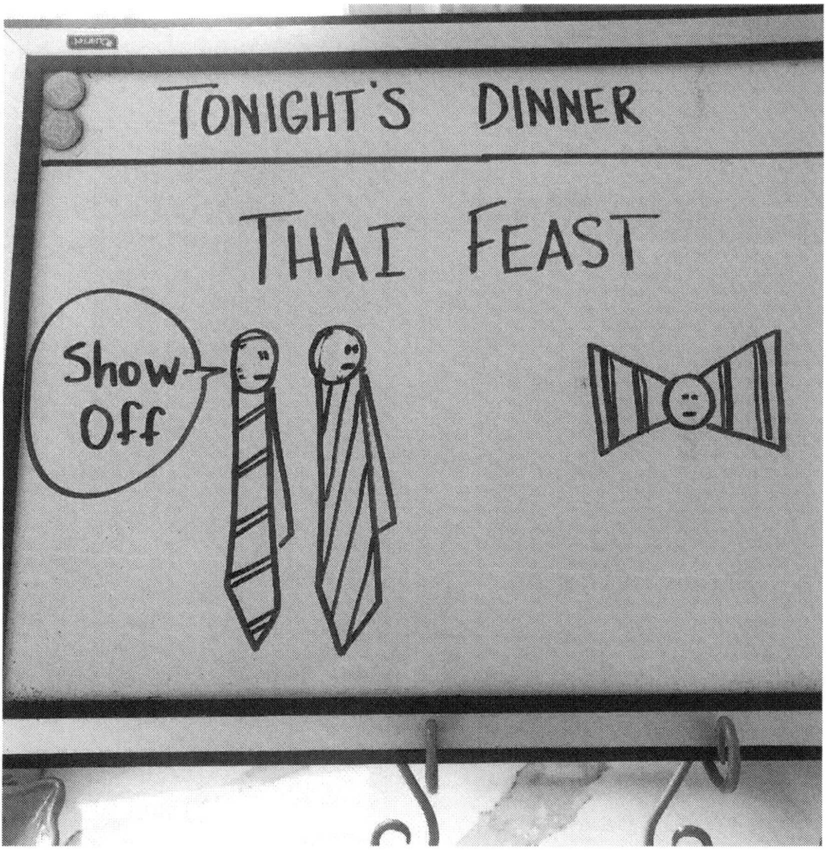
TONIGHT'S DINNER
THAI FEAST
Show Off

#suitandthai

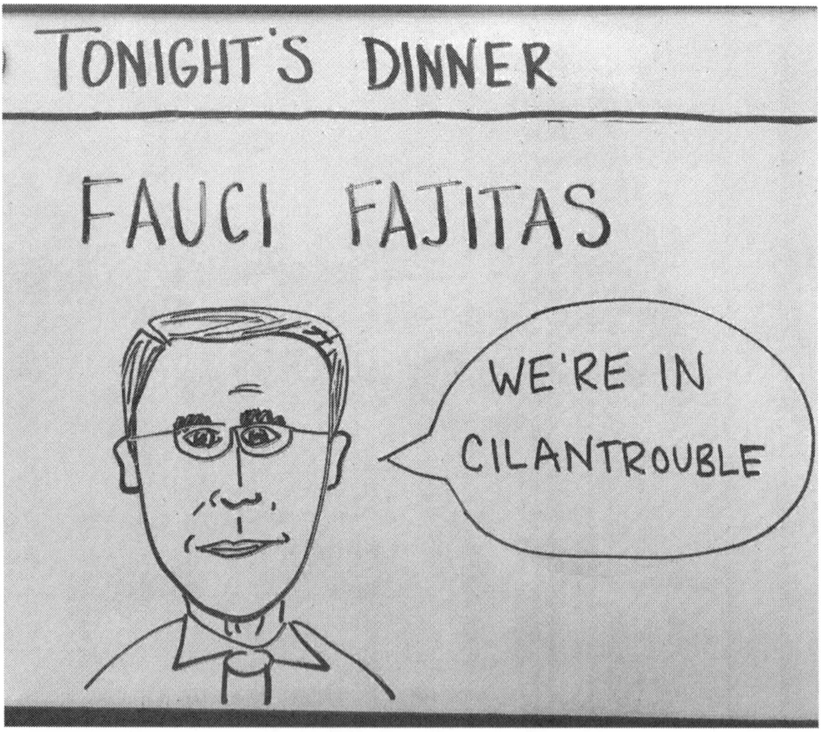
TONIGHT'S DINNER
FAUCI FAJITAS
WE'RE IN CILANTROUBLE

#wearamask

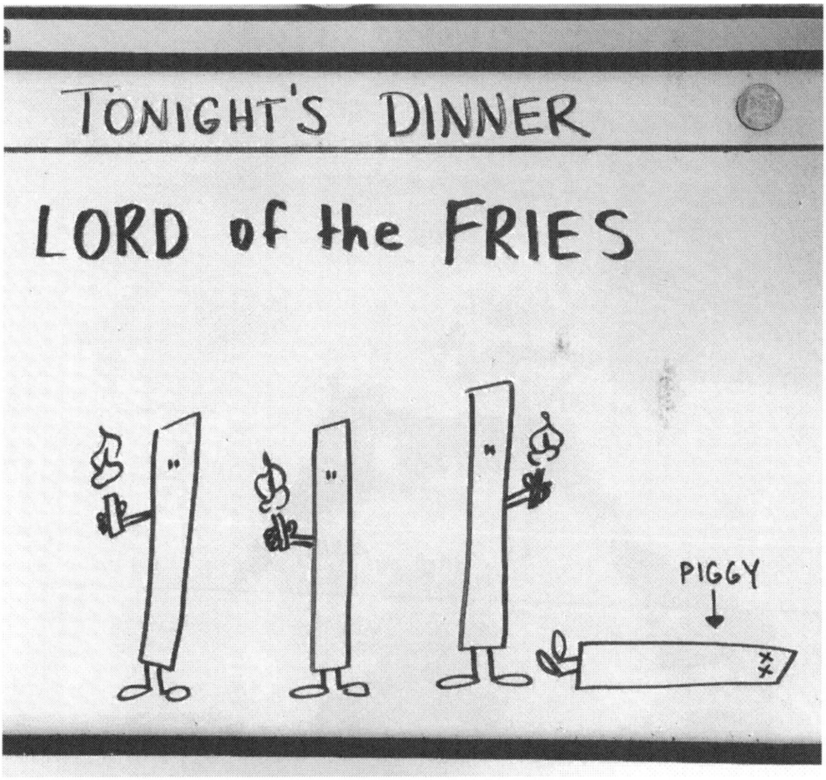
TONIGHT'S DINNER
LORD of the FRIES
PIGGY

#thislittlepiggy

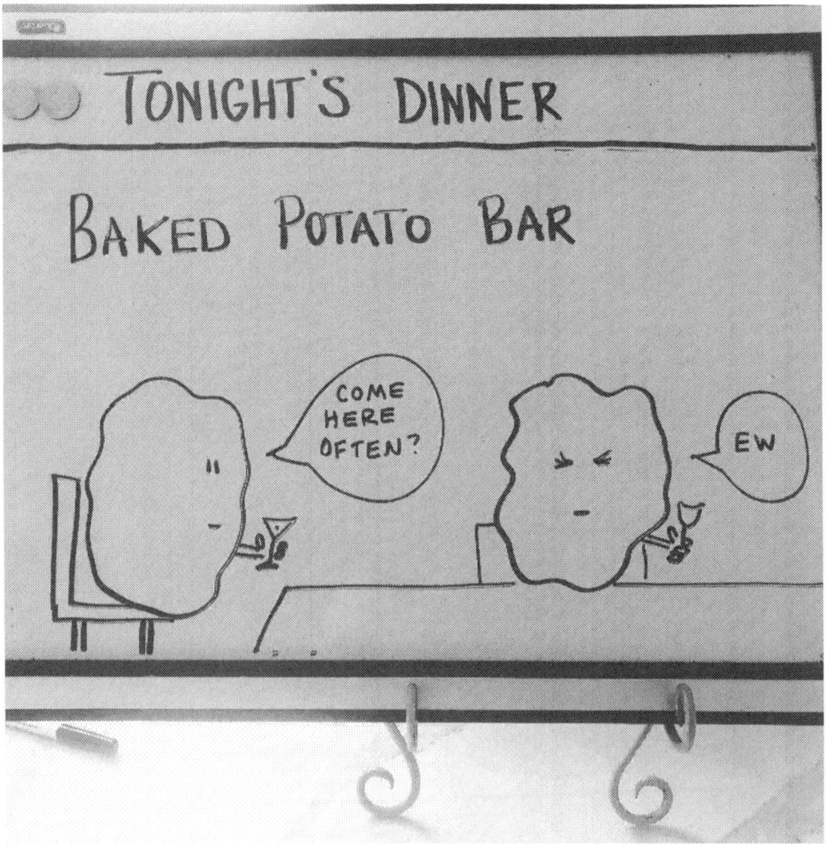
TONIGHT'S DINNER
BAKED POTATO BAR
COME HERE OFTEN?
EW

#hotpotato

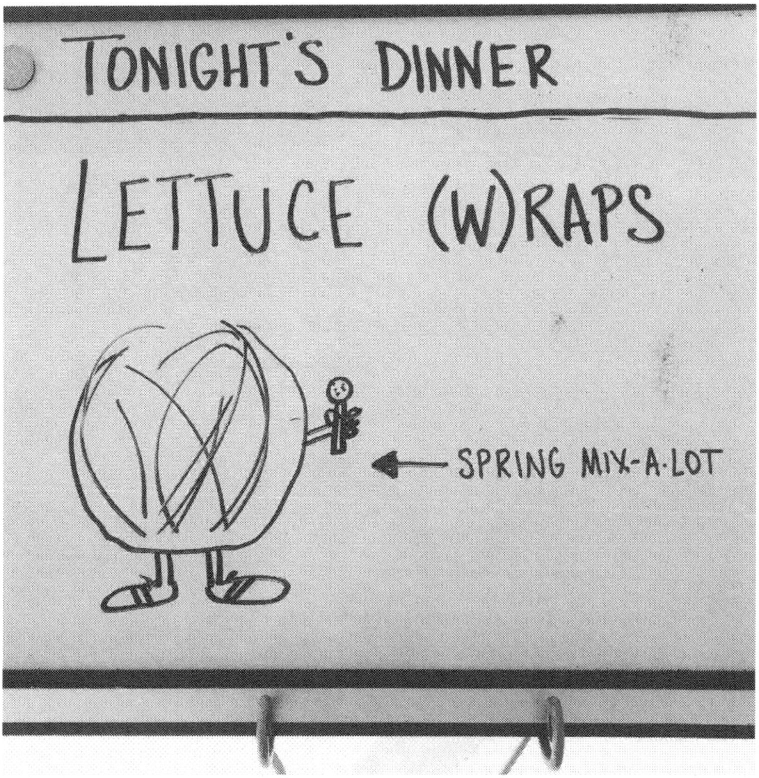
TONIGHT'S DINNER
LETTUCE (W)RAPS
SPRING MIX-A-LOT

#yougetsprung

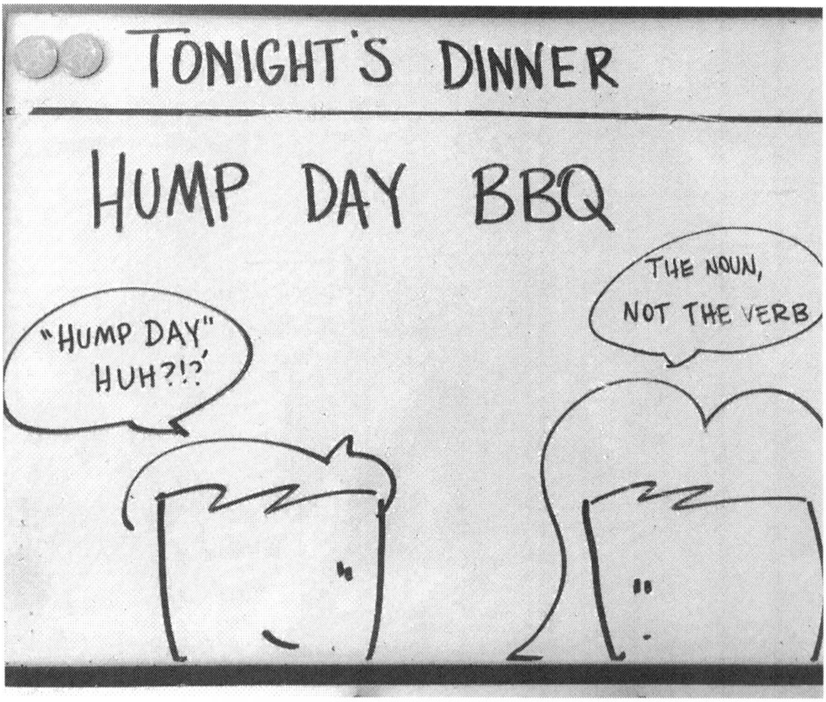
TONIGHT'S DINNER
HUMP DAY BBQ
"HUMP DAY"
HUH?!?
THE NOUN,
NOT THE VERB

#grammarmatters

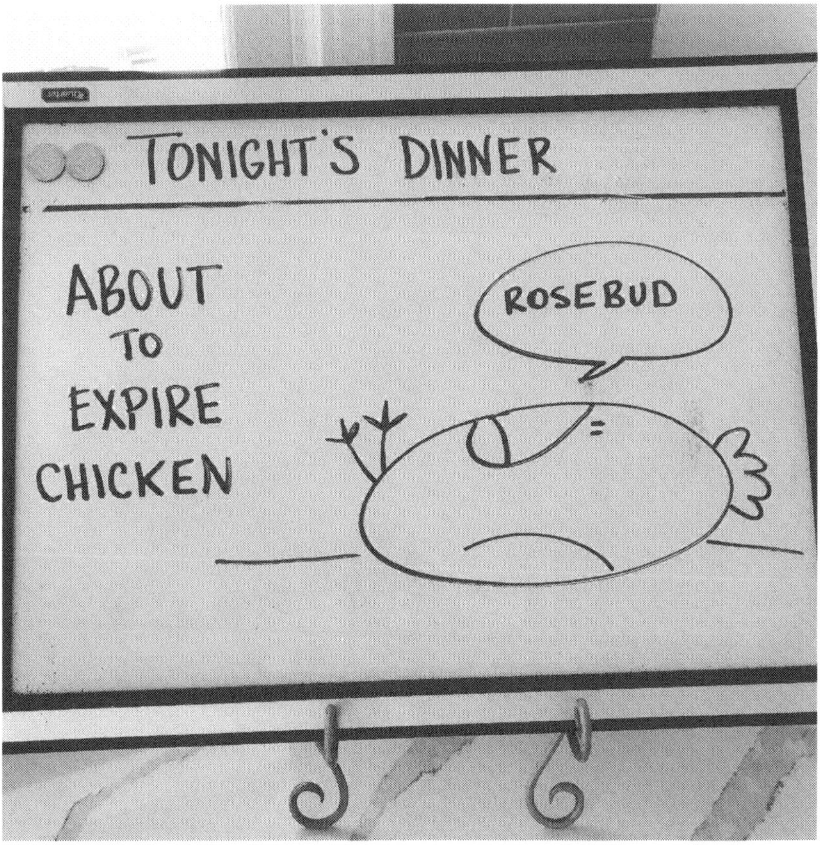
TONIGHT'S DINNER
ABOUT
TO
EXPIRE
CHICKEN
ROSEBUD

#citizenchicken

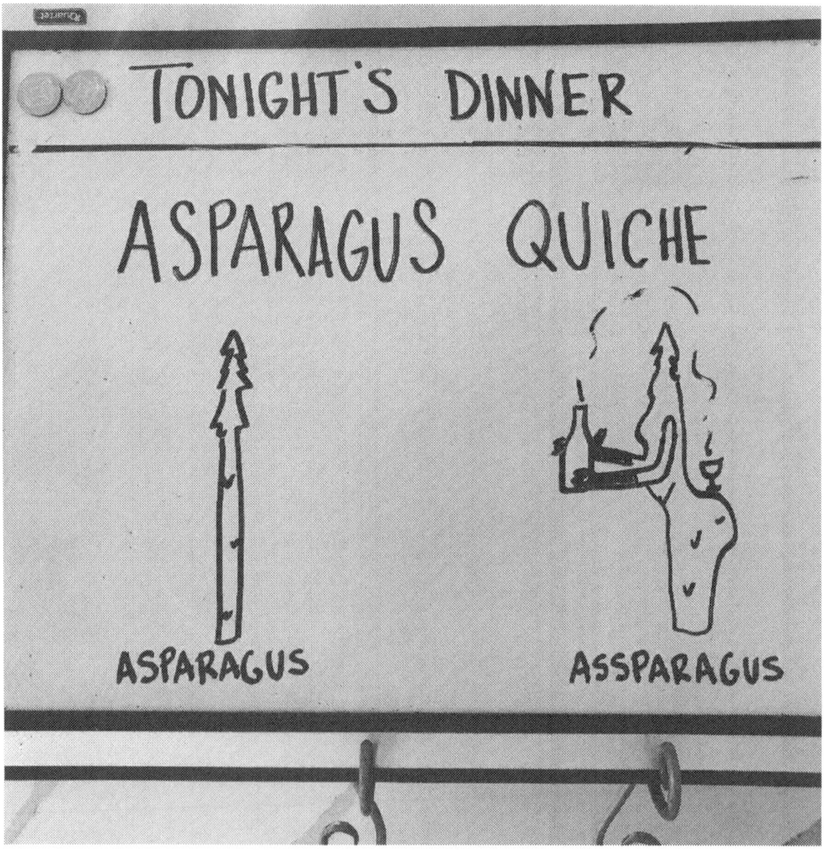
TONIGHT'S DINNER
ASPARAGUS QUICHE
ASPARAGUS
ASSPARAGUS

#quicheandtell

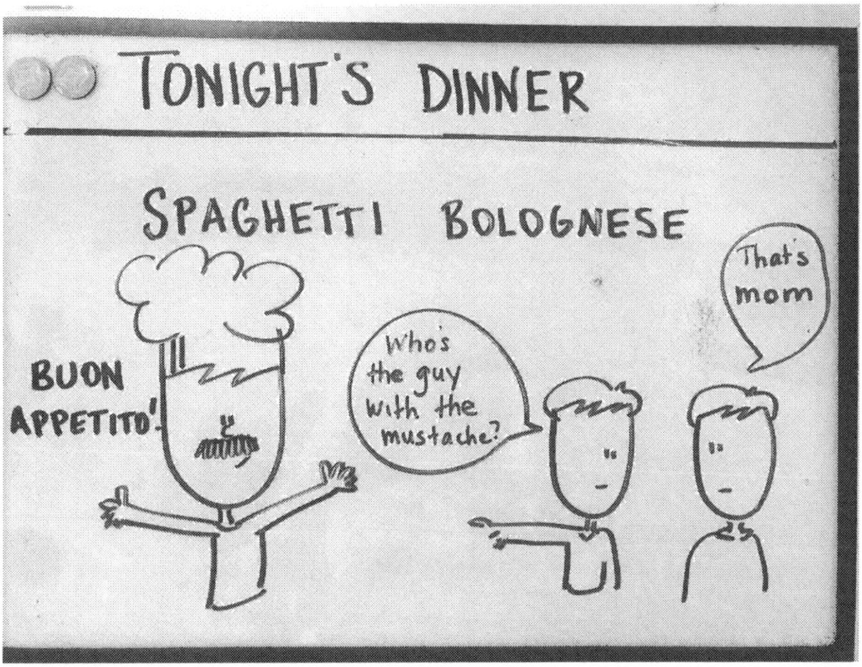
TONIGHT'S DINNER
SPAGHETTI BOLOGNESE
BUON APPETITO!
Who's the guy with the mustache?
That's mom

#thefemaletomselleck

#wonistheloneliestnumber

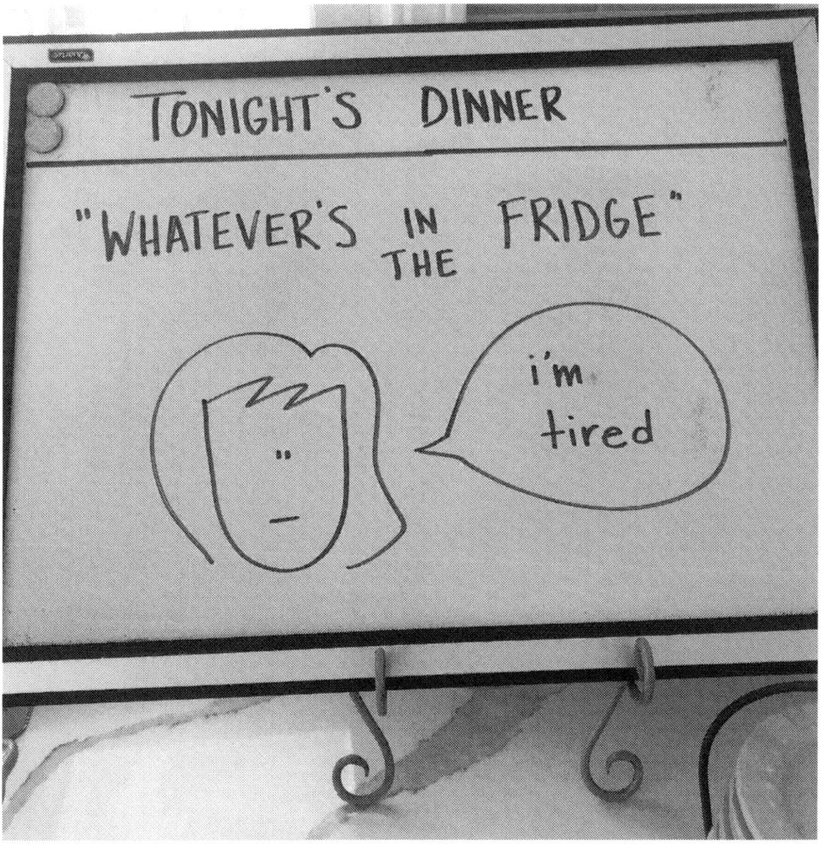
TONIGHT'S DINNER
"WHATEVER'S IN THE FRIDGE"
i'm tired

#thestruggleisreal

#pastathepointofnoreturn

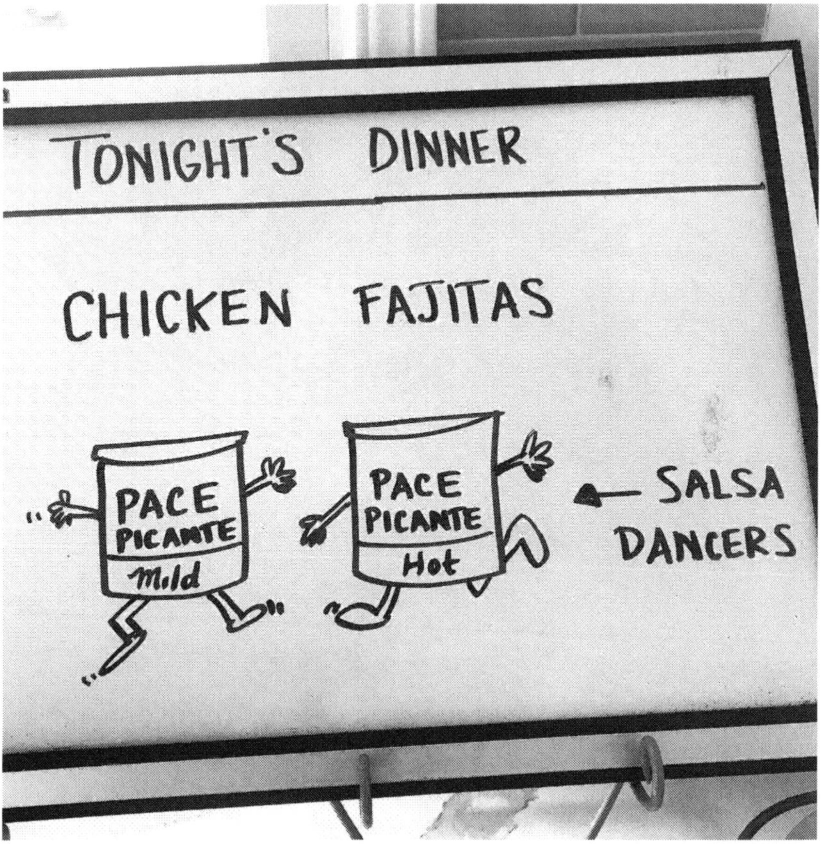
TONIGHT'S DINNER
CHICKEN FAJITAS
PACE PICANTE Mild
PACE PICANTE Hot
SALSA DANCERS

#pickinguptheplace

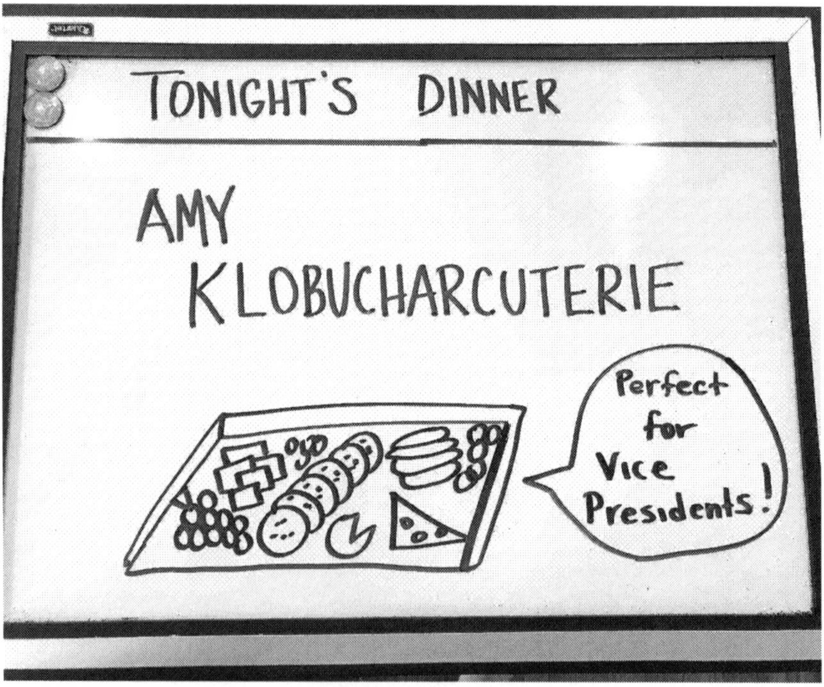
TONIGHT'S DINNER
AMY
KLOBUCHARCUTERIE
Perfect for Vice Presidents!

#saycheese

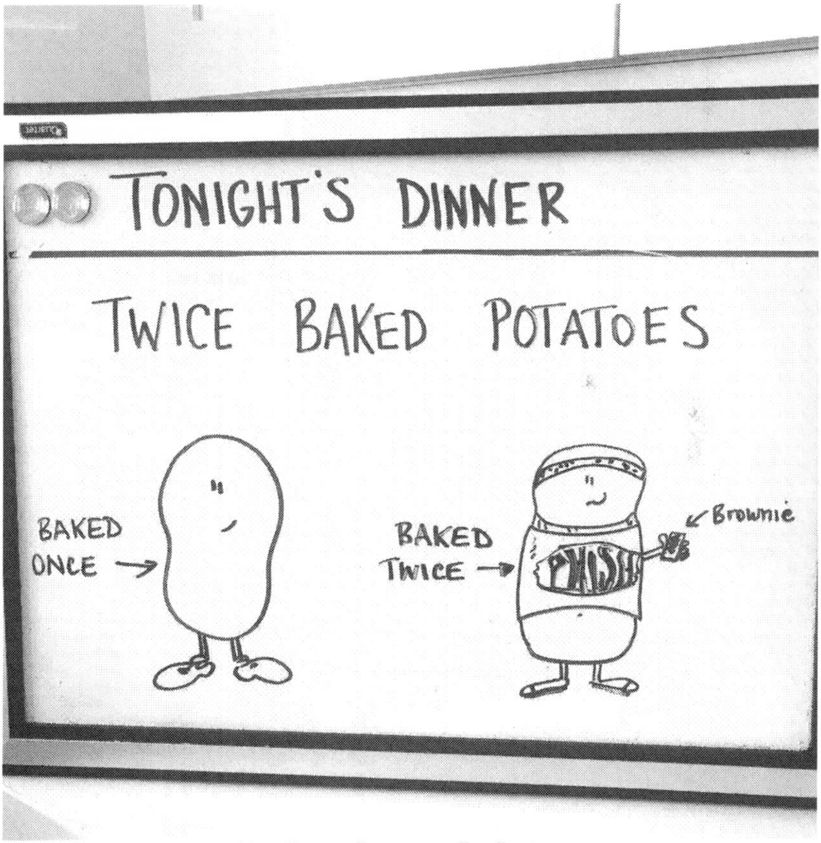
TONIGHT'S DINNER
TWICE BAKED POTATOES
BAKED ONCE
BAKED TWICE
PHISH
Brownie

#phishandchips

#ifithaslettuceitissalad

#paradisebythewhiteboardlight

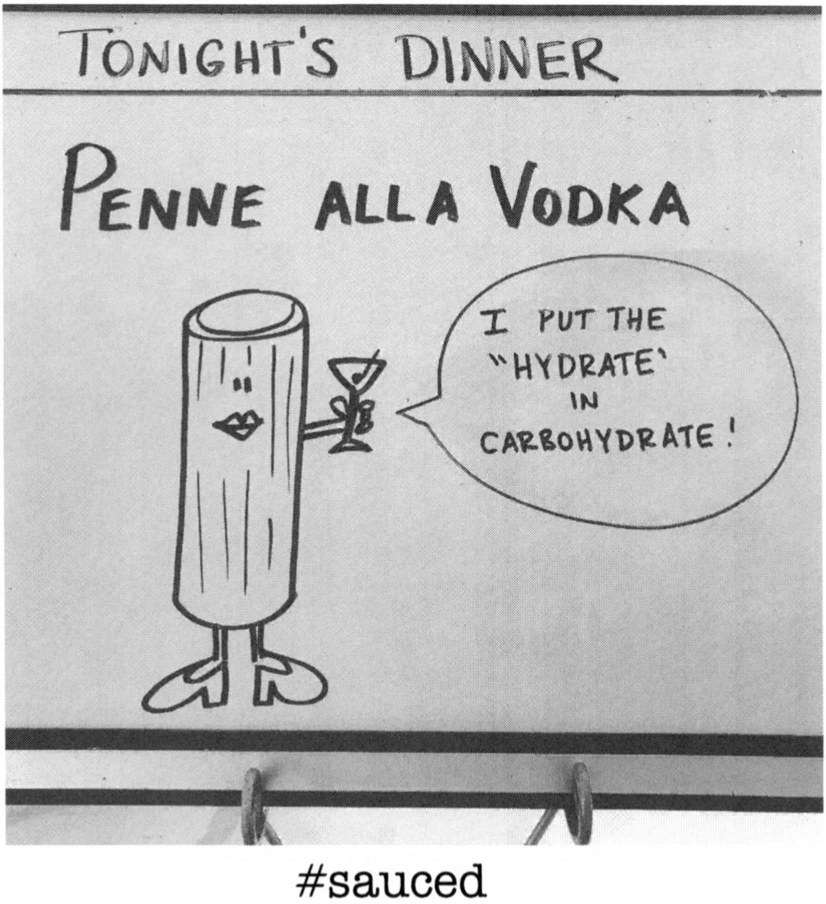
TONIGHT'S DINNER
PENNE ALLA VODKA
I PUT THE "HYDRATE" IN CARBOHYDRATE!

#sauced

#footlooseandfancyfree

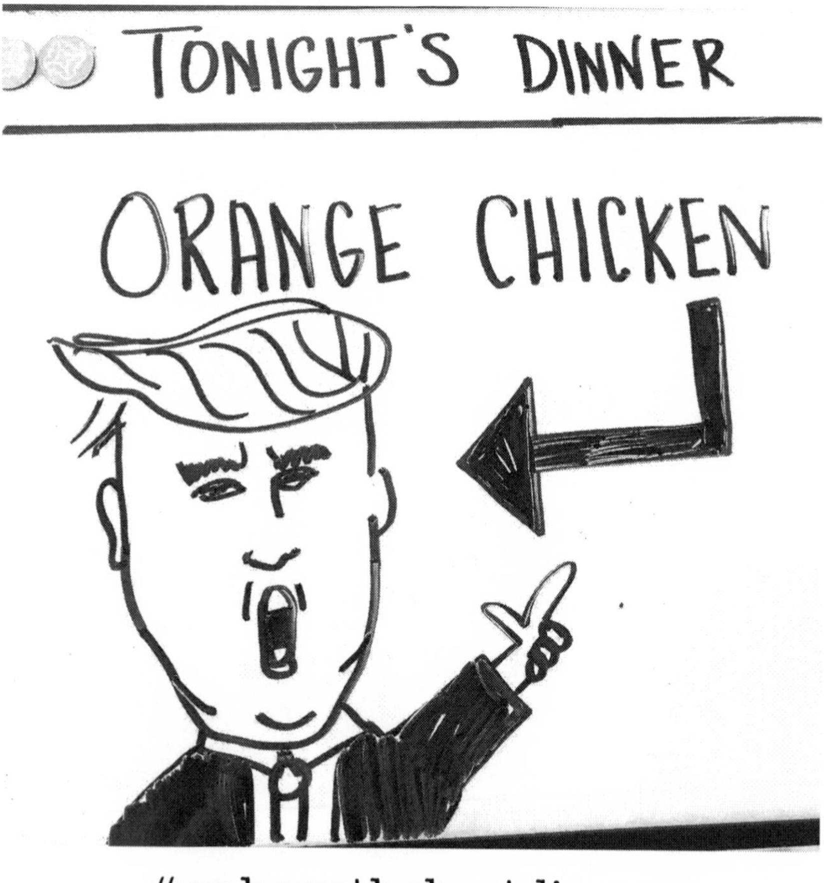
TONIGHT'S DINNER
ORANGE CHICKEN

#wehavethebestdinners

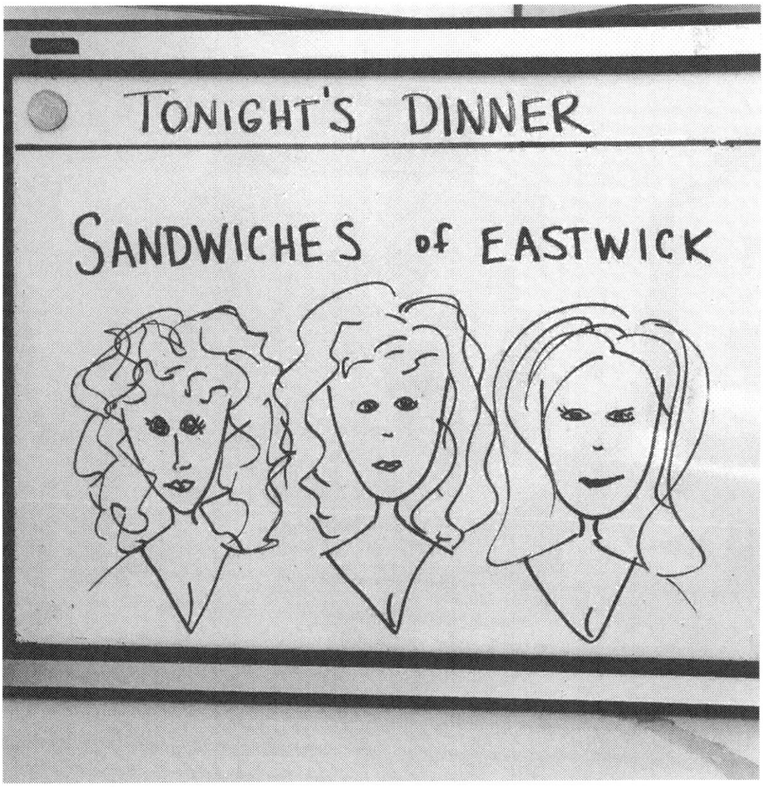
TONIGHT'S DINNER
SANDWICHES of EASTWICK

#ladiesnight

#whambamthankyouyam

#makethemadinnertheycan'trefuse

#solesurvivor

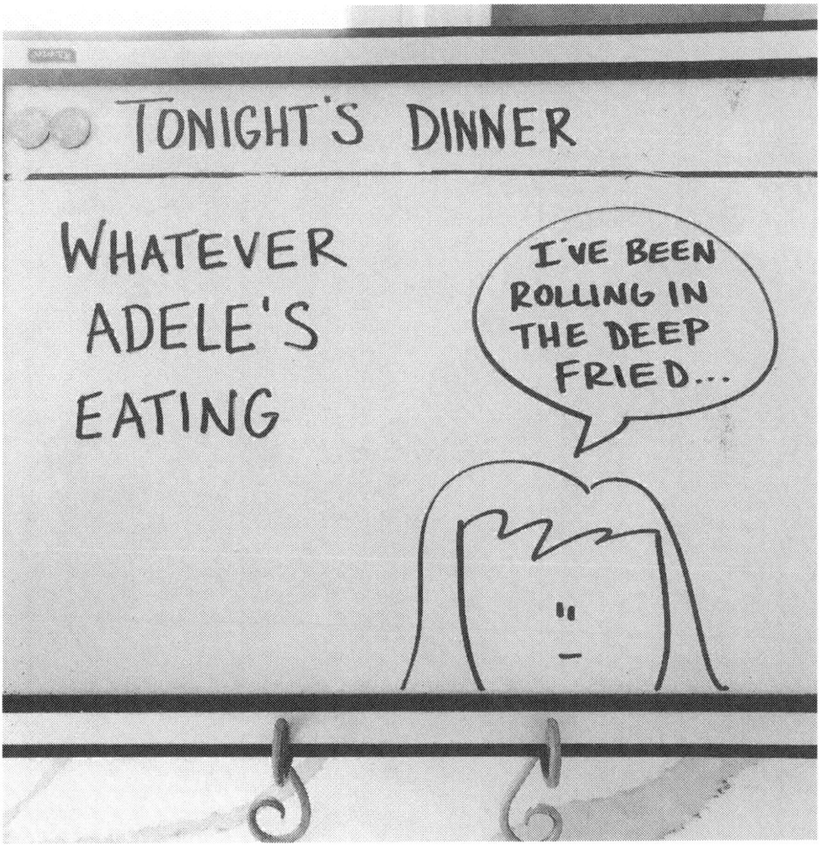
TONIGHT'S DINNER
WHATEVER ADELE'S EATING
I'VE BEEN ROLLING IN THE DEEP FRIED...

#setfiretothegrain

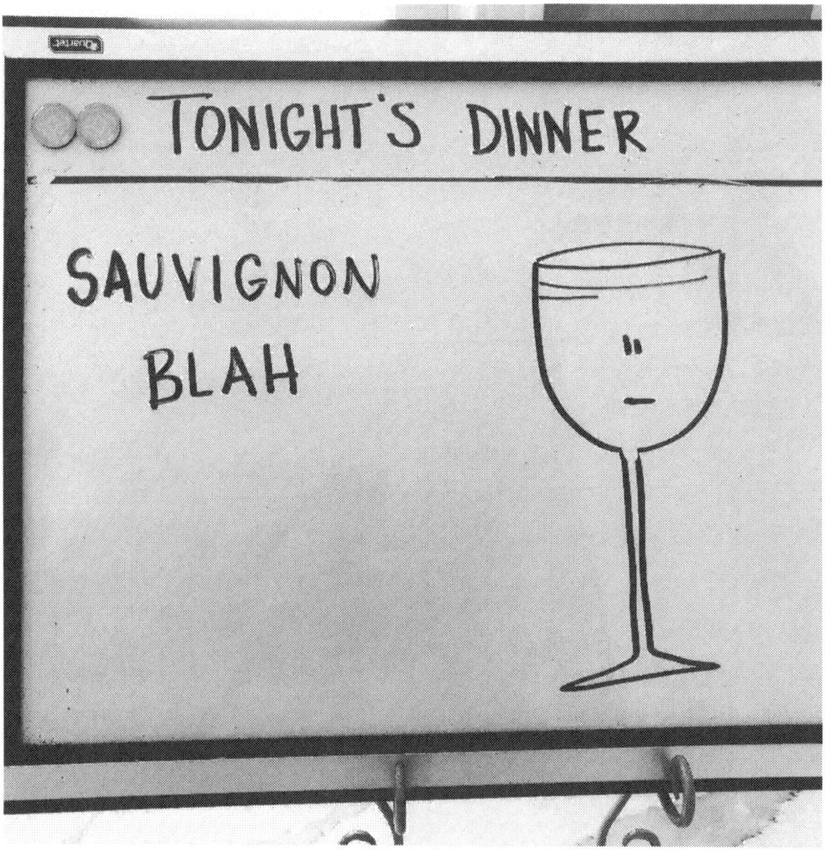
TONIGHT'S DINNER
SAUVIGNON
BLAH

#nowining

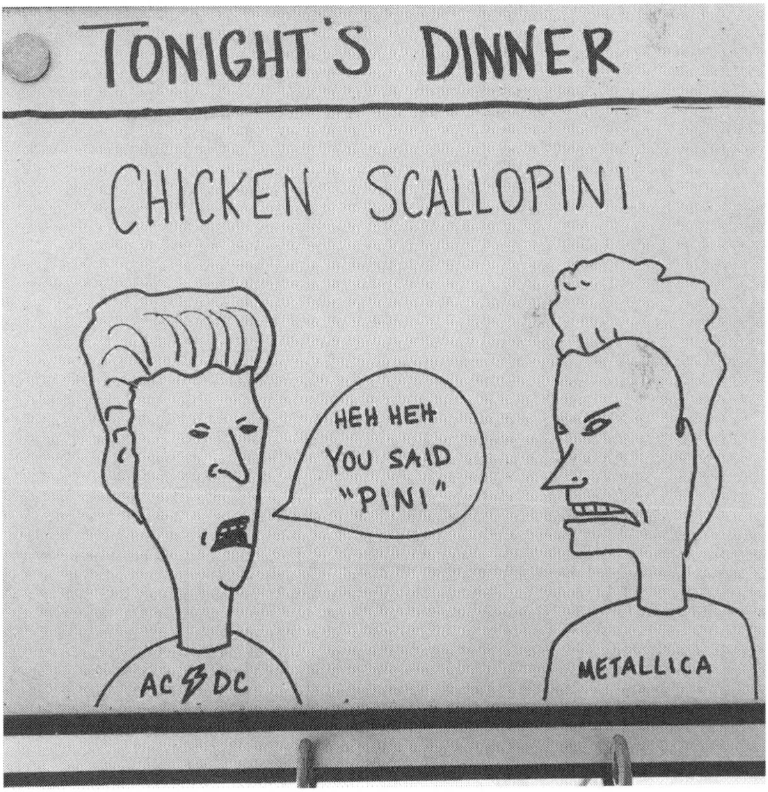
TONIGHT'S DINNER
CHICKEN SCALLOPINI
HEH HEH
YOU SAID
"PINI"
AC DC
METALLICA

#hehheh

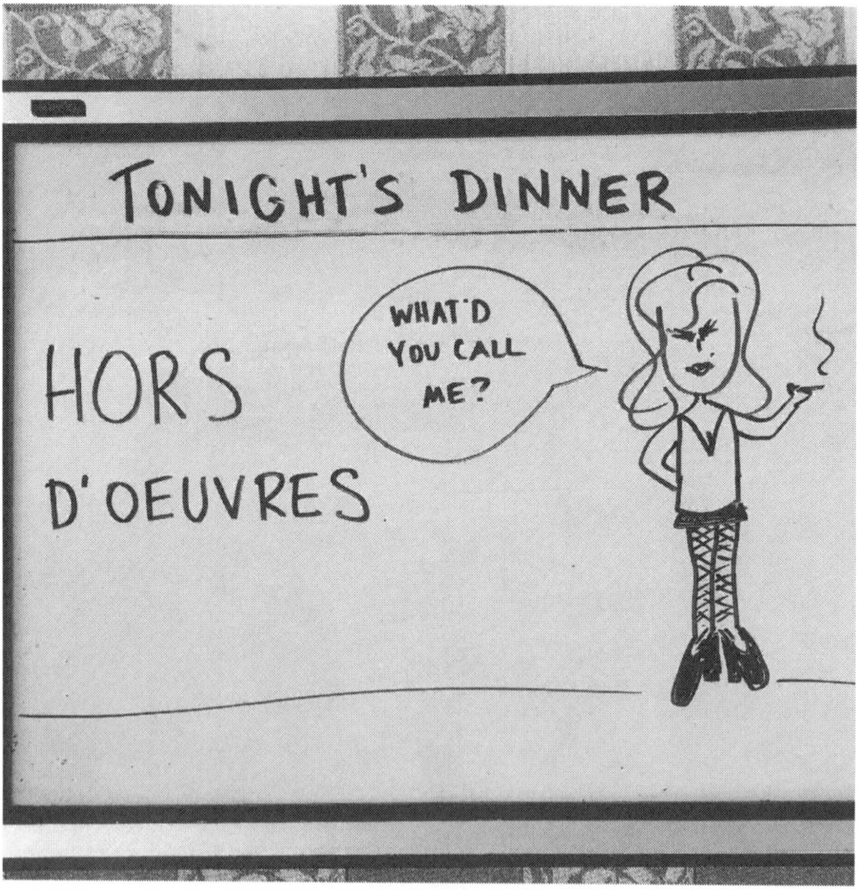
TONIGHT'S DINNER
HORS
D'OEUVRES
WHAT'D YOU CALL ME?

#workinggrill

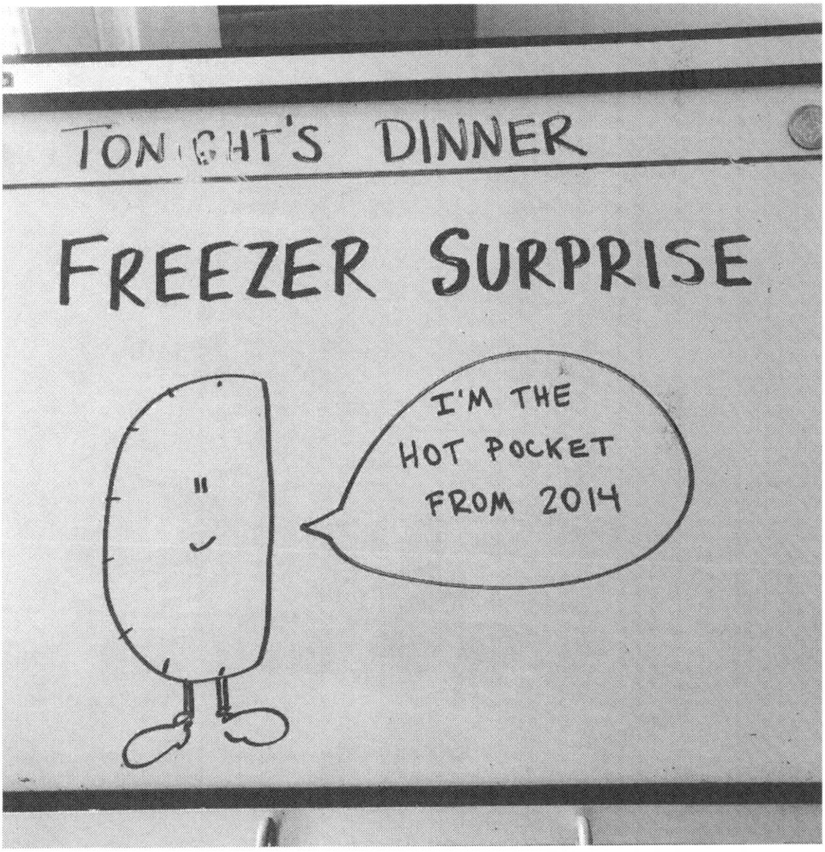
TONIGHT'S DINNER
FREEZER SURPRISE
I'M THE HOT POCKET FROM 2014

#deepfreeze

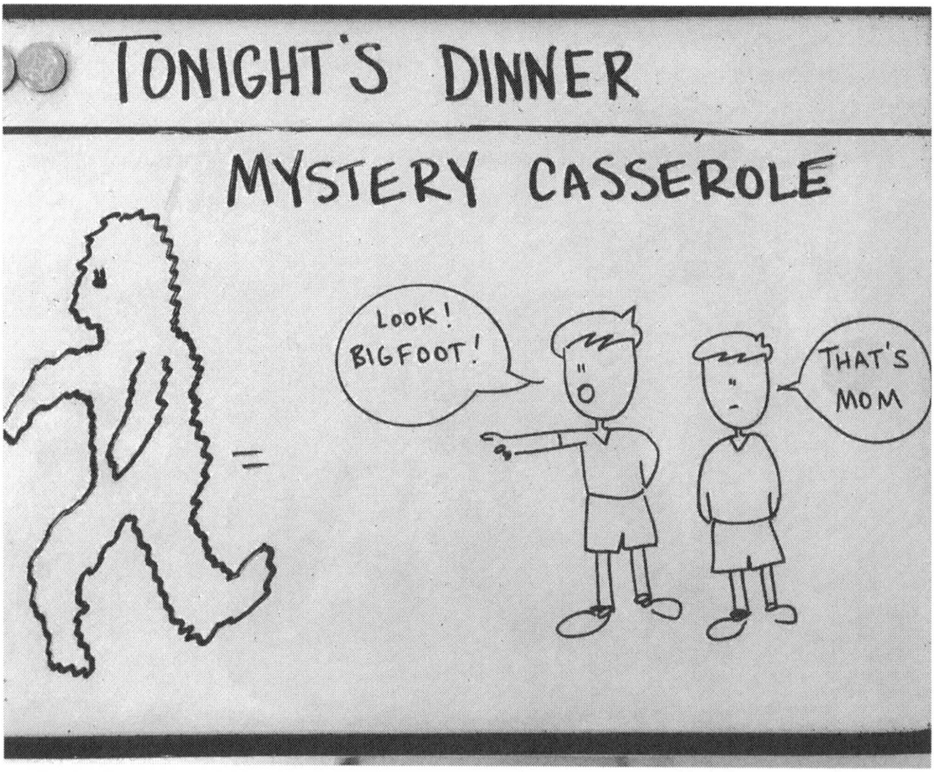
TONIGHT'S DINNER
MYSTERY CASSEROLE
LOOK! BIGFOOT!
THAT'S MOM

#hairapparent

#thereisnopauseinmenopause

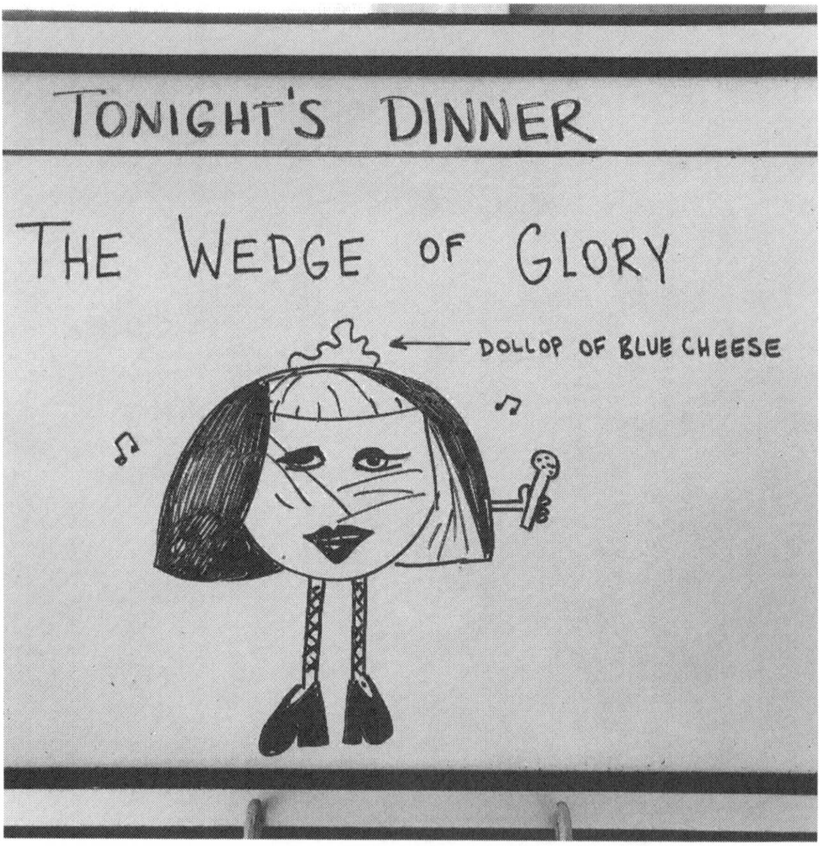
TONIGHT'S DINNER
THE WEDGE OF GLORY
DOLLOP OF BLUE CHEESE

#badromaine

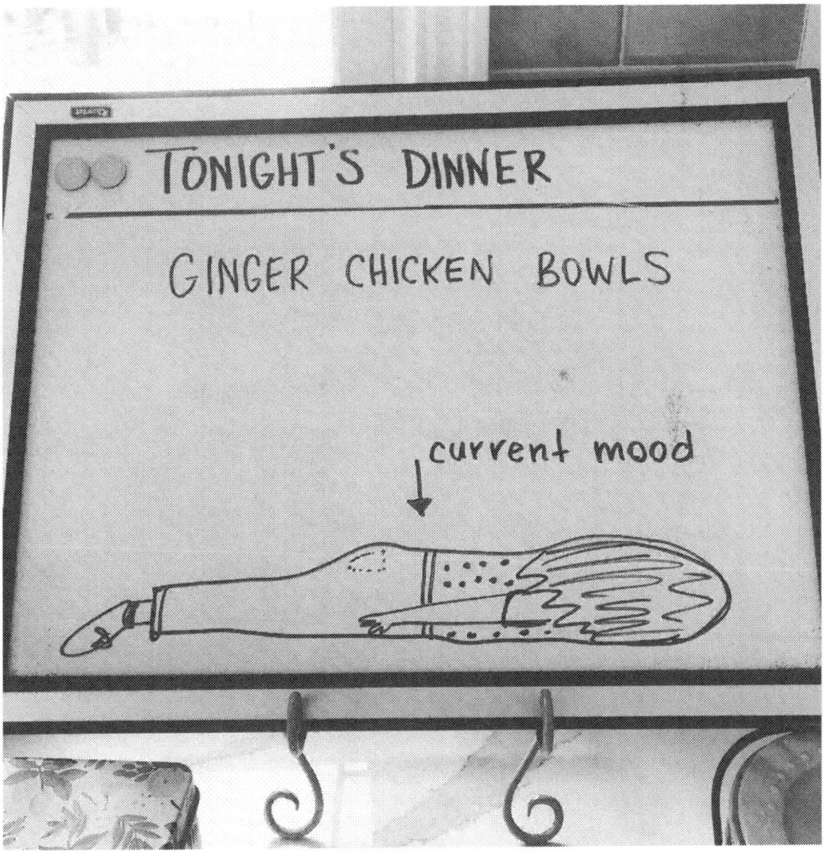
TONIGHT'S DINNER
GINGER CHICKEN BOWLS
current mood

#help

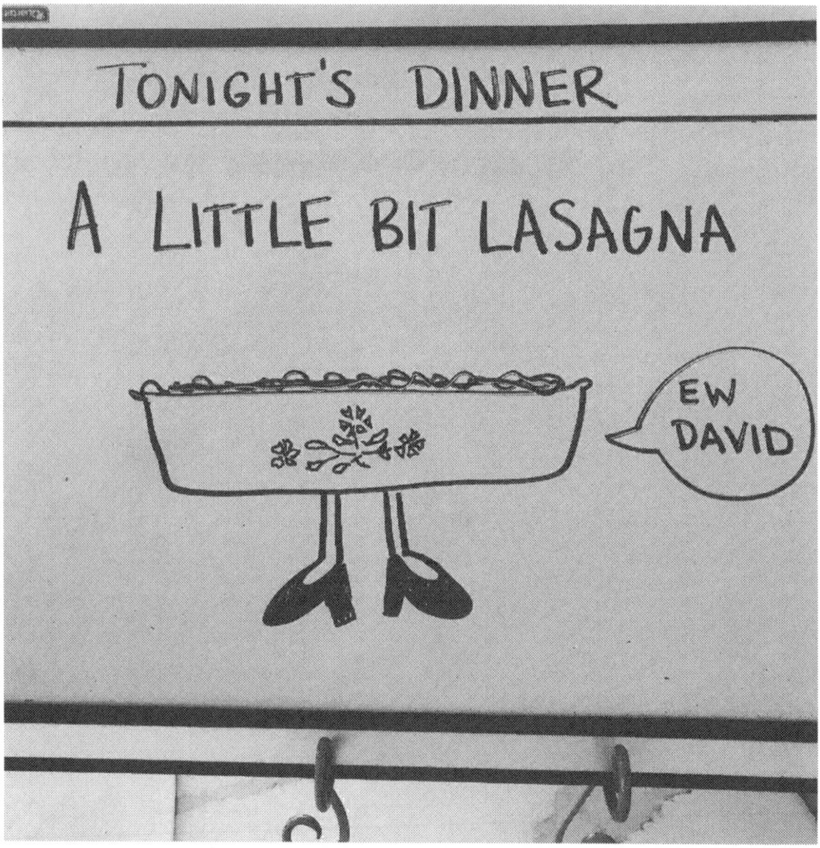
TONIGHT'S DINNER
A LITTLE BIT LASAGNA
EW DAVID

#schittscreek

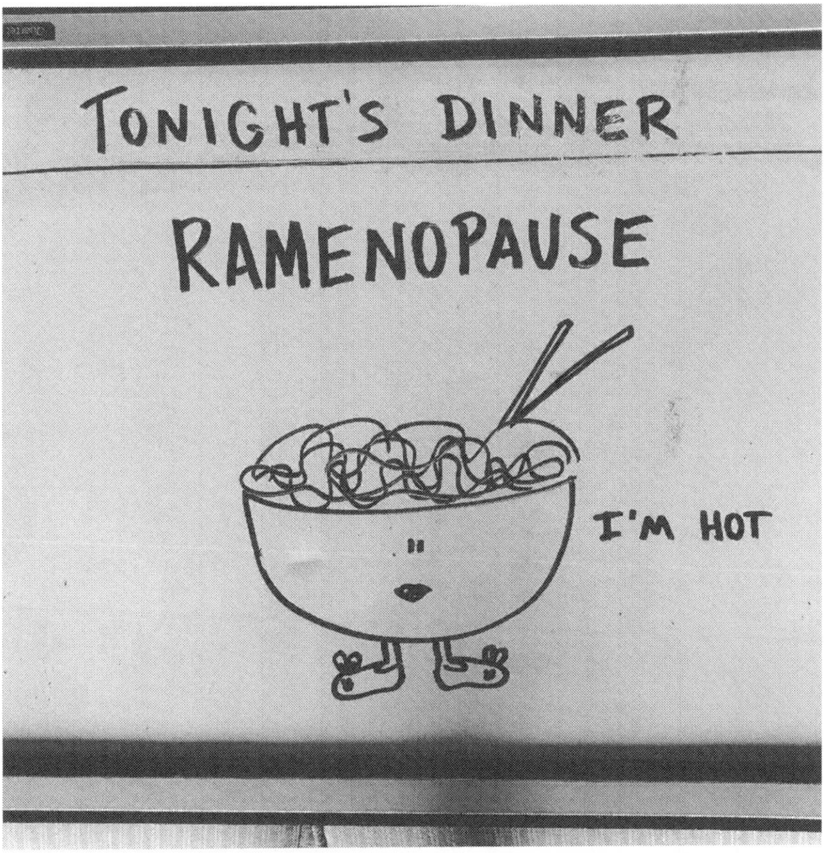
TONIGHT'S DINNER
RAMENOPAUSE
I'M HOT

#hotflashinthepan

#itputsthelinguiniinthebasket

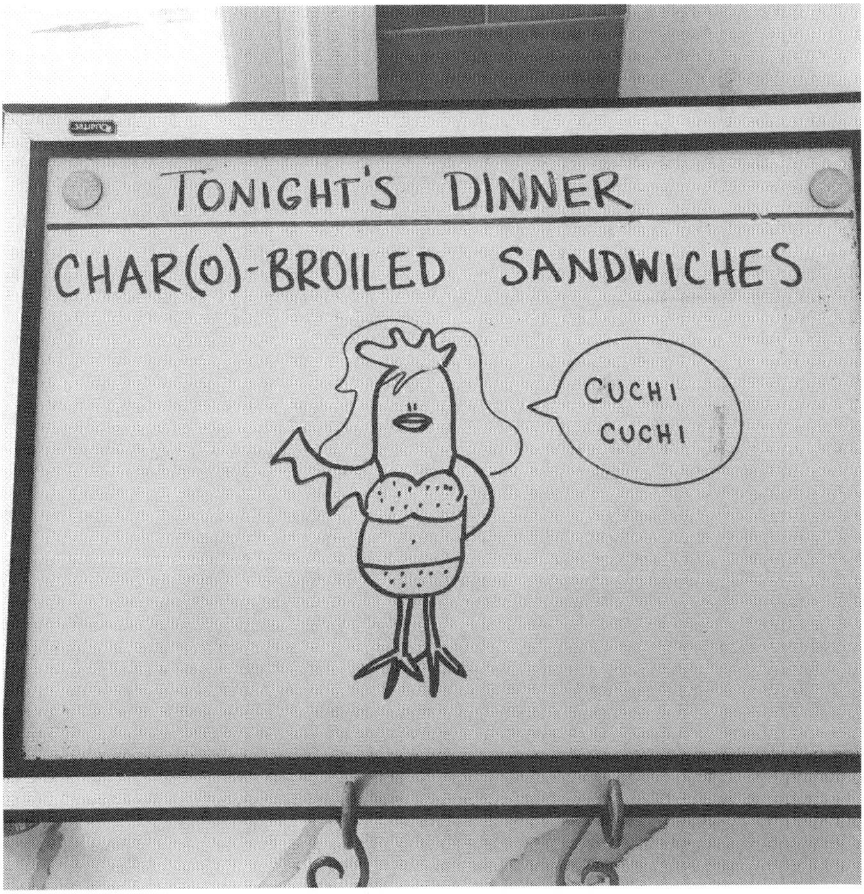
TONIGHT'S DINNER
CHAR(O)-BROILED SANDWICHES
CUCHI CUCHI

#cuchicken

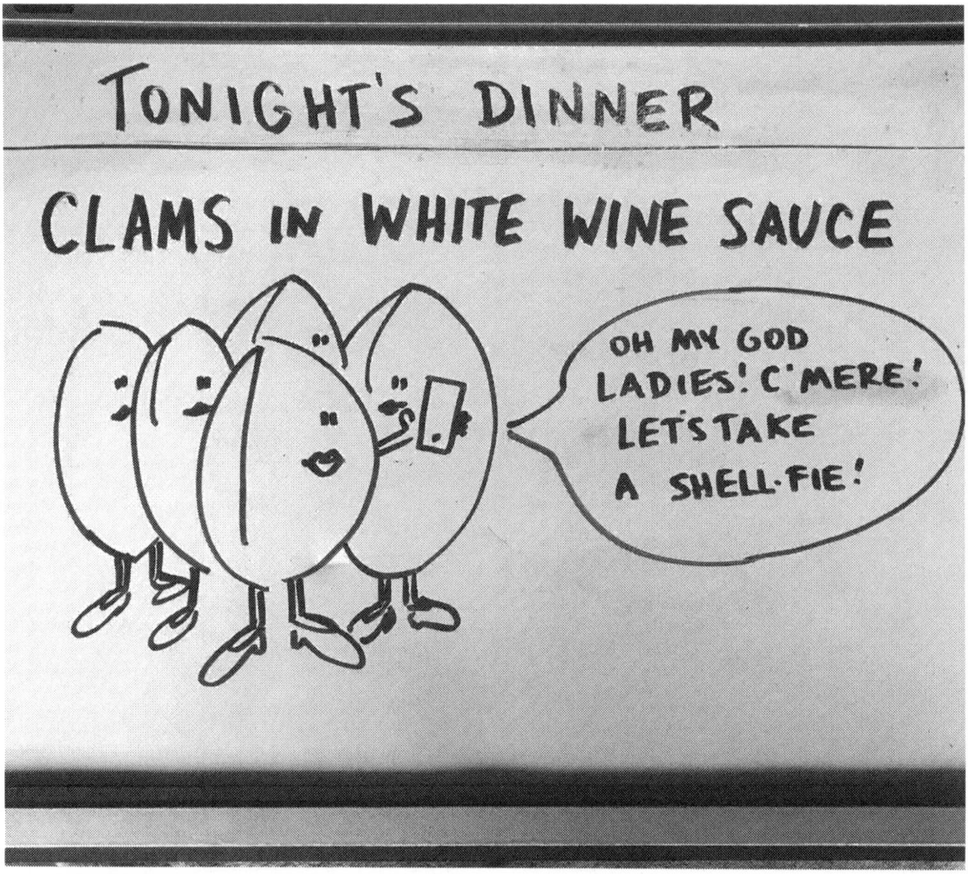
TONIGHT'S DINNER
CLAMS IN WHITE WINE SAUCE
OH MY GOD LADIES! C'MERE! LET'S TAKE A SHELL-FIE!

#instaclam

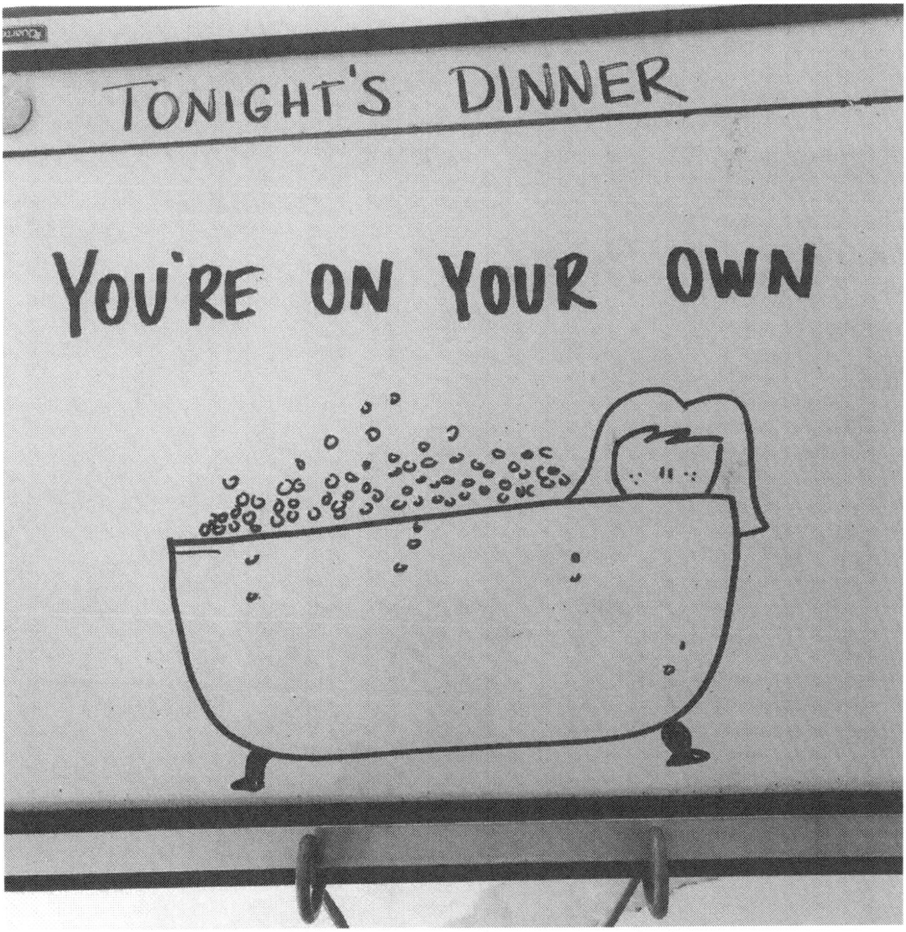
TONIGHT'S DINNER
YOU'RE ON YOUR OWN

#calgonwiththewind

The reviews are in for
COVIDinners: Adventures in
Quarantine Dining

"The best book ever!"
My husband

"It's OK."
My sons

Made in the USA
Coppell, TX
30 October 2020